Songbird

ADELE

Publisher and Creative Director: Nick Wells
Project Editor: Polly Prior
Picture Research: Laura Bulbeck
Art Director and Layout Design: Mike Spender
Digital Design and Production: Chris Herbert

Special thanks to: Jane Donovan, Stephen Feather & Dawn Laker

FLAME TREE PUBLISHING
Crabtree Hall, Crabtree Lane
Fulham, London SW6 6TY
United Kingdom

www.flametreepublishing.com

First published 2012

12 14 16 15 13
1 3 5 7 9 10 8 6 4 2

A CIP record for this book is available from the British Library upon request.

ISBN 978-0-85775-523-0

Printed in China

Songbird

ADELE

ALICE HUDSON

FOREWORD: MALCOLM MACKENZIE,
EDITOR, *WE LOVE POP*

**FLAME TREE
PUBLISHING**

Contents

Foreword

Karl Lagerfeld may have had other ideas, but Adele is the complete package. If she *only* had that incredible voice it would be enough. She would still be a massive star. But she's got the voice, instantly classic songs and here's the kicker that seals the deal in UHU glue: she's the nicest person you'll ever meet.

People bang on about Adele being authentic, but that's not exactly it. Lady Gaga is just as authentic – but Adele is instantly knowable. We understand her. There's no hoopla to distract us from her voice and the deeply personal lyrics that connect with our brains, hearts and, too often, tear ducts.

She has got to be the ultimate crossover artist. Everyone likes Adele. What could put you off? She is emotional without being sentimental, cool, friendly, funny and looks fab without trying too hard. In a world of be-wigged, Auto-Tuned and pitch-corrected pop stars, Adele is a stiff antidote.

I remember the first time I saw Adele sing – because I was drenched to the skin and encrusted in sludge. It was in a tiny tent at Glastonbury in 2007 where, to be honest, most people were seeking refuge from the rain. What a refuge. This unassuming teenage girl flattened the room into silence with an acoustic guitar, a powerful set of lungs and speed dial function into your innermost feelings. It was as if you knew her instantly, and somehow she knew you. And when I finally interviewed her, she didn't disappoint. It was more like a chat round a mate's than the usual teeth-pulling exercise. We didn't swap numbers afterwards and go for shots at T.G.I. Friday's, but hey, you can't have everything.

Malcolm Mackenzie

Editor, *We Love Pop*

Grammy Grabber

In 2009, London-born soul sensation Adele said that to be nominated for a Grammy Award was 'a dream come true' and to win two 'blew my mind.' Fast-forward to the 54th Grammy Awards in February 2012 and the singer was practically staggering as she posed for pictures with six further gongs. She won Record of the Year, Album of the Year and Song of the Year as well as Best Pop Performance, Best Pop Vocal Album and Best Short Form Music Video. The success reflects that of Adele's second album *21* (2011), which easily eclipsed *19*, her debut of 2008. Adele's clean sweep of six Grammys in one night – something only fellow mononymous crooner and Adele fan Beyoncé (Knowles) has ever achieved – was described by the singer as the 'most incredible' night of her life.

'Nothing beats coming home with six Grammys and then coming to the BRITs and winning Album of the Year – I'm so proud to be flying the British flag for all of you.'

Adele accepts her second BRIT Award before being cut off by producers

'I have constant butterflies and goose bumps, it's wearing me out but I LOVE it! I've been sleeping a lot but the minute I wake up, I burst out laughing and it starts all over again.'

Adele's blog, following the 2012 Grammys

BRITs and More

At the BRIT Awards nine days later, Adele was queen of the night again, winning Best British Solo Female Artist and Best British Album for *21*. At the Grammys, she had brought the house down with her soulful, powerful rendition of the hit track 'Rolling In The Deep' and, looking glamorous and radiant, she did so again at the BRITS. Yet when host James Corden was ordered by producers to cut Adele's acceptance speech to a mere two sentences, controversy reigned – not least because of the cockney lass's typical reaction; a one-fingered salute direct to the cameras. Adele was quick to let the world know the gesture was aimed at the 'suits', not fans. In fact, the organizers were forced to issue a public apology.

Following the album *21*, Adele took home a whole host of prestigious awards, including three American Music Awards (Best Pop/Rock Album, Best Pop/Rock Female Artist and Best Adult Contemporary Artist) and two AIM Independent Music Awards, recognizing artists signed to independent record labels in the UK. At the Music of Black Origin Awards (MOBOs), she was named Best UK R&B/Soul Artist, and she also picked up a BT Digital Music award, MTV's Song of the Year award (for 'Rolling In The Deep'), four MTV and MTV Europe Video Music Awards and dozens of other nominations. She has graced the covers of many major magazines, including *Rolling Stone*, British *Vogue* and *Glamour* (which also named her UK Musician/Solo Artist of the Year in 2011).

On The Up

With two award-winning, critically acclaimed albums and a massive international fanbase, 2012 sees Adele's star shining brightly. But following the release of *21*, the future looked uncertain as problems with the singer's voice threatened to ruin her career. She recovered well from throat surgery in November 2011, by which time she had even found a new love. Now she is in a good place and has publicly promised a new album soon – one more upbeat, with not a trace of 'bitter witch' as she herself terms it. The girl who grew up in tiny flats in less well-heeled parts of London has also moved herself into a £2 million beach house after experiencing phenomenal commercial success. When the BRITS was screened, *21* shot back up two places to No. 1 in what would be its 57th week in the UK charts. Having broken countless records, it is the eighth biggest-selling album ever in the UK. Despite cancelled tour dates, Forbes estimates the singer made US$18 million in 2011. Adele herself has noted, 'It's been the most life-changing year.'

'*All the categories were full of people I adore, with brilliant songs, records and performances, so not in my wildest dreams did I think to actually prepare anything proper to say just in case.*'

Adele, post-Grammys

'I love Adele. I don't imagine that anyone could come down here and say they don't love her, love her story, love her success, love her songs, love her humanity, love her voice, love her dirty jokes – I just think she's fantastic.'

Kylie, red carpet interview, BRIT Awards 2012

The Voice

Despite initial comparisons to her fellow Londoner, the late Amy Winehouse, and other female soul acts – Adele has been likened to everyone from the late Whitney Houston to a combination of Joni Mitchell and Carole King – there's no denying she is now widely thought of as a unique talent. 'I keep getting called "the new Amy Winehouse" and things like that,' she told a reporter in 2008 after her first album, *19*, began to attract attention. 'It doesn't bother me – I'm the biggest Amy fan there is, but when people hear more of my music, they'll realize we're not alike.'

Adele's five-octave contralto has been described by critics as 'soulful', 'rare' and with a 'bluesy husk', while her performances are noted to be 'spine-tingling', 'stunning' and 'electrifying'. Music bible *Rolling Stone* said her sound was 'a mix of soul power, tender sweetness and scary emotional transparency'. There can be no doubting the talented, pitch-perfect vocalist has wide appeal. Her anguished break-up songs were quick to prove themselves in having significant crossover success as far as building a fanbase was concerned. Adele was the highest-selling artist of 2011, despite having to cancel a good portion of her tour dates after suffering a devastating vocal cord haemorrhage. According to *Vogue*, the success was largely because the album dabbled in R&B, soul, hip-hop, jazz and country, so managed to cross over 'to nearly every musical radio format save classical'.

Keeping It Real

Adele's distinctive sound is coupled with a dramatic yet relatively static performance style. There are a few well-timed hand gestures, and buckets of emotion conveyed in her face, as well as through her powerful, soulful voice. The singer told *Vogue* as part of the October 2011 cover story – she has twice featured on the magazine's cover – that she had never given much thought to the presentation of her songs: 'I definitely think less is more. I don't think I could pull it off, doing an elaborate show.' She admits her album contains 'a couple' of tracks worthy of 'a few explosions and dancing teams and stuff', however she remains adamant that she would feel 'really uncomfortable' displaying her music in that way, professing, 'I just want to sing it.' While she loves watching other female performers such as Lady Gaga and Katy Perry shake their booties and dance like athletes, for her iit's different: 'I don't want to perform with my body.'

Bawdy Broad

Adele is well known for her on-stage, often-bawdy banter. She has an easy, cheeky charm, a distinctive cockney accent and is notorious for cussing like a sailor, even during interviews. But her BRIT finger gesture was not the first time she has flipped the bird on live TV. During an interview with Fox in 2009, she managed to flash an illustrative middle finger as part of an answer to the very first question. *The Observer* dubbed her 'Mighty Mouth'.

'As soon as I got a *microphone* in *my hand*, when I was *about 14*, I realized I *wanted to do this*. Most people don't like the way their *voice sounds* when it's *recorded*. I was just so *excited* by the *whole thing* that I *wasn't bothered* what I *sounded like*.'

Adele

During live gigs she will often explain what each song's about, telling the audience about the time in her life it relates to – her chat is described by *Vogue* magazine as 'blistering and hilarious.' The singer has admitted to always playing the part of 'the joker' and being overly loud. She is the sort of person you could easily envisage as a stand-up comic and yet, despite her seemingly endless supply of confidence, Adele says it's often nerves fuelling her non-stop stage banter as she still suffers from stage fright. 'Behind the eyes it's pure fear. I find it difficult to believe I'm going to be able to deliver,' she admits.

'I didn't really realize I had a natural sense of humour until I started telling stories onstage – you get the timing down. Also, people laugh when I open my mouth anyway, even if I don't tell a joke, because they are laughing at my accent.'

Adele

Who Do You Love?

Adele was just three years old when she attended her first live gig with her mother: a Cure concert in London's Finsbury Park. It was the same year her father, a Welsh plumber, left her mother, practically severing all ties with his daughter in the process. After that first gig, the tot took to the music straight away and it was an obsession that stuck.

'I've got no problem explaining what my lyrics are about. I really like poetry – I'm not very good at reading it, but I love writing it. Singers like Jill Scott and Karen Dalton are amazing, proper poets.'

Adele

As a young girl, Adele was all about pop. Her all-time favourite band were the all-dancing, all-singing, mega 'girl-power' group, The Spice Girls. From the age of seven, she was a die-hard fan. She told *Now* magazine in 2011 that, even though being a Spice fan might be seen as somewhat 'uncool' today, she would never feel ashamed to admit loving them. Indeed,

she went so far as to say, 'They made me who I am.' She even attended their comeback gig in 2007 and had a ball – 'Seeing them was just like being a little kid again.' The experience may even have brought back fond family memories (Adele has said she used to love impersonating The Spice Girls for the entertainment of her mother's friends at dinner parties). As a youngster she was also a big fan of boy bands – Take That, Backstreet Boys and N-Sync were favourites. Britney Spears was another idol. Today, Spears is one of many artists to have professed their love of Adele. 'Her voice is just amazing. She has this soulful sound that rings with you and stays with you.'

R&B

When she was 11, Adele and her mother moved from North to South London, setting up home first in Brixton, then neighbouring West Norwood. With the move came a shift in the music she listened to. Now it was all about the new-style R&B popular at the time. Favourite acts as a pre- and young teen included Aaliyah, Destiny's Child, Mary J. Blige, Alicia Keys, LL Cool J and 'Puff Daddy or P. Diddy, or whatever it is he calls himself.' Indeed, Adele describes Lauryn Hill's album *The Miseducation of Lauryn Hill* and Alicia Keys' *Songs in A Minor* as 'life-defining'.

The music-loving teen began attending gigs and, music-wise, seeing global phenomenon Pink perform at her local Brixton Academy was a big deal. 'It was the *Missundaztood* record, so I was about 13 or 14,' recalls the star. 'I had never heard,

'I don't consider myself a singer. My favourite singers are Etta James and Aretha Franklin. If you were to look up the word singer in the dictionary, you'd see their names. Not mine.'

Adele

being in the room, someone sing like that live [...] I remember sort of feeling like I was in a wind tunnel, her voice just hitting me. It was incredible.'

'I was so in love with Mike Skinner, I wrote him a letter and when I told my friend about it, she cussed me. So I went and pretended to do the washing up and cried.' Adele

Soul

Another defining moment came around the same time, when she inadvertently picked up an Etta James record. At the time, she was passing through a very brief American rock phase, according to *The Guardian*. Yet she fancied James' glamorous hairdo and bought the compact disc to show her hairdresser the picture. Some time later, she popped the CD into her player and was instantly in love: 'She [Etta] was the first time a voice made me stop what I was doing and sit down and listen. It took over my mind and body.' Adele believes it was a 'natural progression' for her to get into soul artists such as James, Aretha Franklin and other artists, whom she describes as the 'legends of the proper R'n'B – Rhythm and Blues rather than contemporary auto-tuned R&B.' Other acts she admires include Jill Scott, Billy Bragg, Peggy Lee and Jeff Buckley.

'She fell pregnant with me when she would have been applying for uni, but chose to have me instead. She never, ever reminds me of that. I try to remember it.'

Adele credits her mother

London Girl

Adele Laurie Blue Adkins was born on 5 May 1988 in Tottenham, a deprived part of North London with a high rate of unemployment. Her mother, Penny Adkins, was just 18 and an art student when her daughter was born. Adele's father, Mark Evans, exited Adele's life when she was aged three, leaving mother and daughter to fend for themselves. The singer has had limited contact with him since. Now living in Cardiff, the former alcoholic has yet to really know his child. Adele was openly furious when she found out that her dad had sold a story about their relationship to *The Sun* tabloid in 2011. In the article, Evans talks of courting Adele's mother, stating, 'For me it was love at first sight.' He told the newspaper he asked Penny to marry him but that she had turned him down, saying she was too young.

Not A Daddy's Girl

Evans even seemed to link himself to his daughter's extraordinary talent by suggesting he was responsible for Adele's musical taste: 'After Adele was born, I'd lie on the sofa all night, cradling her in my arms and listening to Ella Fitzgerald and Nina Simone. I'm certain that is what shaped Adele's music today.' While he concedes in the same interview that Adele would 'probably snort' at the afore-mentioned suggestion, he professes how much he regrets having been a self-described 'rotten' parent. Following

publication of the article, the singer said publicly that she wanted nothing to do with him. She suggested she was on the brink of forgiving her father for the past when he sold out. In typical Adele style, she declared she would 'spit in his face' if she ever saw him again, stating he had no right to talk about her and that he didn't even know her. She would later use the same 'spit in his face' tactic when expressing her anger towards her ex-partner.

Moving Around

As a young, single woman with a daughter to support, Penny Adkins worked various jobs. The tight little family unit moved around often, depending on work. Penny's former vocations included masseuse, furniture maker and office administrator. Adele has spoken of her mother's large family being a big bonus while growing up. 'My mum is one of five and everyone's got kids and all the kids have started having kids, so when I say nieces and nephews I mean my second cousins really,' she told *Vogue*. 'Mum's side is massive. All brilliant. Dominated by women and all really helping each other out, so even though she brought me up on her own, it was kind of a team effort.' Adele credits her large extended family with making her such a strong force: 'You had to fight to get your voice heard because everyone was screaming and chatting at the same time.'

Although born in North London, she spent much of her childhood south of London's famous Thames. Time was spent in Brixton (known for being a rough area) before the pair

'I did little concerts in my room for my mum and her friends. My mum's quite arty – she'd get all these lamps and shine them up to make one big spotlight. They'd all sit on the bed.'

Adele

moved into a small flat above a discount store in neighbouring West Norwood. Mother and daughter also spent two years in the city of Brighton in East Sussex. Despite attending no fewer than 10 different schools, Adele loved moving house. 'I think that's why I can't stay in one place now. My mum always made it fun,' she told *Rolling Stone*.

'*Mum loves me being famous! She is so excited and proud as she had me so young and couldn't support me, so I am living her dream. It's sweeter for both of us.*'

Adele

Best of BRIT-ish

As a schoolgirl, Adele had music constantly on the brain. She even persuaded her mother to make her a sequined eye patch to wear to school so she could channel pop star Gabrielle. Adele's natural musicality saw her take up clarinet and guitar, but her ultimate devotion was reserved for vocals. She used to queue for hours to get into recordings of the Saturday morning chart show *CD:UK* and was a big Top 40 fan from an early age.

'The kids were passionate about what they were doing there, whereas the ambition at my state school was to get pregnant and sponge off the government. That ain't cool.'

Adele

Adele's family isn't musical, yet the young songbird was certainly encouraged at home. By the age of 12, she had decided she wanted to be a professional singer. 'We'd be watching *The X Factor* and my family would

> '*The [school music] teacher was a bit rubbish. They gave me a really hard time – trying to bribe me, saying that if I wanted to sing I had to play clarinet to sing in the choir. So I left.*'
>
> *Adele*

tell me I should go on,' she recalled. 'But then you'd see a parent on the show, saying "My child is the next Mariah," and the kid would be rubbish. So I'd look at them and think, F*** you, you just want me to be embarrassed for a good laugh.' She continued singing for family and friends. One family friend – a dance producer – declared her voice 'wicked' and invited her to record a cover of Blondie's 'Heart of Glass'. As soon as the microphone was in her hand, Adele truly knew her calling.

School Sucks

At high school in South London, Adele got to hang out with the R&B kids and 'sit around the playground singing'. Yet it was a rough place, even by London standards. In addition, she found pursuing music in the way she desired impossible. Cheeky Adele made her desire to sing and perform her own songs clear, but her teachers insisted she play clarinet and sing in the choir. Luckily, Adele's talent at the tender age of 14 was enough to secure her a place at The BRIT School for Performing Arts and Technology in Croydon, just south of London. Despite its excellent reputation, The BRIT School wasn't Adele's first choice though. She had wanted to attend Sylvia Young Theatre School in central London because one of the Spice Girls – 'Baby Spice' Emma Bunton – had trained there, but her mother couldn't afford the fees. As the BRIT School does not charge tuition fees for any lessons contained within the compulsory curriculum, this was the next best choice.

Just Like 'Fame'

Adele greatly preferred her new learning environment, despite an admission to early misgivings. 'If I hear someone's from stage school, I'd think they were a d***head,' she once said. Luckily, there were no 'jazz hands' and no compulsory dancing, as she had feared: 'It had free rehearsal rooms and free equipment, and I was listening to music all day, every day, for years. The music course was really wicked.' Adele has likened the atmosphere to the 1980 movie *Fame*, with pupils 'having sing-offs in the foyer.'

A persistent punctuality problem almost got her kicked out though. 'I'd turn up for school four hours late. I wasn't doing anything, I just couldn't wake up,' she told *Rolling Stone.* Sleeping in yet again but this time on the day of a key performance sparked a change. Devastated, she instantly learned a key lesson in professionalism and gave up her tardy ways – 'My heart exploded in my chest. It was pretty horrible – now I'm always on time.' At BRIT School, Adele found herself surrounded by talent and her classmates (class of 2006) included Jessie J, Leona Lewis, Kate Nash and Luke Pritchard and Hugh Harris, current members of indie band The Kooks. Amy Winehouse also attended The BRIT School for a year in 2001. Later, after Amy's tragic death in 2011, Adele would sing a moving version of 'Make You Feel My Love' at the Greek Theater, Berkeley, California, in tribute.

'I'm the biggest Amy [Winehouse] fan there is. If I was compared to someone I didn't like then I'd be annoyed, but I think so highly of Amy it's nothing but a compliment.'

Adele

'There were *some people* at *school* who really *pushed hard* – you could tell they really *wanted it*. *Adele* never really had that, but she was a *great performer* and *everyone* would be *completely silent* and in *awe* when she *performed*.'

Former classmate and current guitarist, Ben Thomas

Out Loud

Adele's initial break came after she recorded a trio of demos as part of her final year's coursework at the beginning of 2006. A pal uploaded them on to Myspace, and very soon they attracted views and the attention of record companies. The only label Adele had heard of was Virgin and naturally, an email from a rep at XL Recordings aroused suspicion – 'I thought it was just some perv on the Internet, so I emailed back and said, "Leave me alone, I'm organizing my birthday party." He asked if I was signed, and I told him no and that he could email me in a few weeks when I was finished school.'

She had no idea that the label's signings included Radiohead, Dizzee Rascal, The White Stripes and M.I.A. As soon as she clicked at the initial meet, just after her eighteenth birthday in May 2006, she became 'f***ing excited'. She had been so concerned about the legitimacy of the professed record company employee's email, she took a male friend to the first meeting for security. Negotiations progressed quite quickly from there. 'We met, they liked me and signed me. I feel bad telling that story because it was really that easy,' Adele confessed to *Cosmopolitan*.

Done Deal

Adele needed a manager and so Nick Huggett at XL recommended Jonathan Dickins, founder of September

Management. She liked him as he made her laugh 'like literally, stomach cramps the next day'. He also had British singer/songwriter Jamie T on his books – Adele was a big fan. Dickins signed a contract with Adele in June 2006 (the XL signing was made official three months later).

Around this time, the singer decided to stop partying and really knuckle down. She told *Elle* that playing her worst gig ever – one of her first – at an East London pub had sparked the decision. All her friends and family were there, plus another 300 were seeing her for the first time. She hadn't realized how late she was due to perform and by 2 am, she'd downed far too many – 'I played three songs, I forgot the words and I fell off my chair. It was a free show, thankfully. Can you imagine paying to see someone forget their own lyrics and fall off their chair? Worst thing ever!'

Showstopper

With an initial goal of releasing a successful single set firmly in her mind, Adele had no idea of the amazing journey that lay ahead. She immediately set to work, recording vocals for a song called 'My Yvonne', which featured on the 2007 debut album of another of Dickins' clients, Jack Peñate. Adele would eventually contribute to Peñate's second album too. 'She came in and killed it,' Peñate has said of their studio time. 'Her voice always makes such an impact on anything because it's the most beautiful thing.'

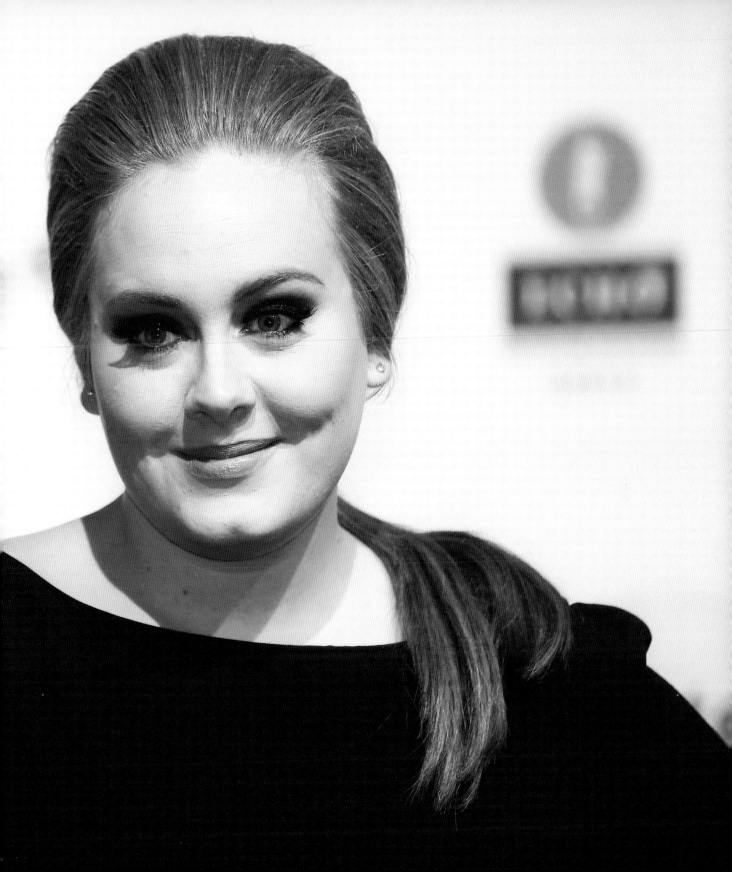

Early Gigs

Adele continued to support other acts and played smaller London venues, where she often accompanied herself on acoustic guitar. *Observer* writer Tom Lamont wrote of seeing her at the Scala in London's King's Cross as a complete unknown on the bill, faced with a restless, noisy crowd. Yet he recalls that she instantly captivated the audience, silencing them with her performance and he knew then that he was witnessing real talent. The year 2007 also saw her support former Pop Idol winner Will Young at the MENCAP 'Little Noise Sessions', a charity concert at London's Union Chapel. Her breakthrough track, 'Hometown Glory', was released in October that year. It was written by the singer aged 16 as a tribute to the city she loves after her mother tried to persuade her to move to Liverpool for university.

'I made my guitarist – Ben – come along to my first meeting with XL Recordings. He's puny, Ben – looks like a dwarf – but I'd never heard of XL so I thought I might be on my way to meet an Internet perv or summink.'

Adele

'The crowd were agitated and noisy and truth be told, quite bored. Then Adele walked on stage with an acoustic guitar and a beer, and tamed the belligerent room in an instant.'

Tom Lamont of The Observer recalls the first time he saw Adele

Rising Star

Following the release of 'Hometown Glory', anticipation for Adele's first album began to mount seriously. A big moment for Adele was when the producers of BBC2's *Later... With Jools Holland* got in touch after viewing her material on YouTube. They invited her to appear on the show, which she did in August 2007 – alongside former Beatle Paul McCartney and Björk, no less. It must have been somewhat nerve-wracking for the young singer to perform her ballad 'Daydreamer', yet as noted by *The Observer*, her performance charmed the audience, the gig easily recognizable as a key point in her career. Her reputation continued to climb and, on 4 January 2008, it was announced that Adele had been tipped as the No. 1 predicted breakthrough act of the year by Sound of 2008, an annual BBC poll of 150 of the UK's most influential music critics, reviewers and editors.

More Than A Voice

Adele's a sensational singer, yet she is a talented songwriter too. Indeed, her desire to write was firmly cemented when Shingai Shoniwa of UK indie band The Noisettes moved in next door during her second year at The BRIT School. Adele could hear her through the walls – 'I'd go round and we'd jam and stuff like that. Just hearing her and her music really made me want to be a writer and not just sing Destiny's Child songs.'

'She's just brilliant; I don't think there's any science to it. She is possibly the best singer, or one of the best singers, I've ever heard in my life. That voice is incredible.'

Jonathan Dickins, Adele's manager

For Adele, however, writing is difficult, if not inspired – 'Something has to completely take over my life for me to write about it; it's the only time I shut up.' Most of the tracks on her first two albums were inspired by events and feelings brought about by failed romances. Some were written in the full-on heat of the moment – like 'Chasing Pavements', composed just a few hours after she learned her boyfriend of six months had cheated. He was out drinking when she found out. She went to the bar he was in, punched him in the face and was promptly thrown out. As she wandered the streets alone aimlessly, she began to wonder what she was doing and came to the conclusion she was 'chasing an empty pavement'. By the time she got home, the lyrics and melody were recorded on her mobile phone, at which stage she sat down and arranged the chords.

Stage Fright

As her star continued to rise, Adele had to become used to playing for larger and larger audiences. She may appear confident now, yet the singer has revealed that to this day she suffers terribly with stage fright. 'When I hear artists say, "Performing is what I'm meant to do," I think Whaaat? This ain't what you're meant to do, it ain't normal!' She has spoken of feeling 'scared' of audiences and admits the fear has led to more than one embarrassing incident – 'One show in Amsterdam I was so nervous, I escaped out the fire exit.

Once in Brussels, I projectile vomited on someone.'
She has said she can bear performing but doesn't
enjoy touring due to these anxiety attacks. The panic
attacks have been so intense for Adele that she has
turned down big festival gigs in the past and expressed
her preference to have smaller, intimate venues booked,
despite the reduction in income.

Adele also hates flying, yet the singer is friendly and
unguarded in interviews and has gained considerably in
confidence since she was first photographed as a wide-eyed
19-year-old. She's now a media regular, having appeared
on *Letterman*, *Ellen* and *60 Minutes* and performed on
The X-Factor, as well as having made appearances on the
cover of all the major magazines, such as *Vogue*, *Elle*, *Marie
Claire* and *Rolling Stone*.

*'I've tried to write about friends'
problems or fictional things
and I can't do it because I have
to connect with what I'm singing
about, or it ain't good for me.'*

Adele on songwriting

*'I get so nervous onstage, I can't
help but talk; I try. I try telling my
brain, stop sending words to the
mouth, but I get nervous and turn
into my grandma.'*

Adele

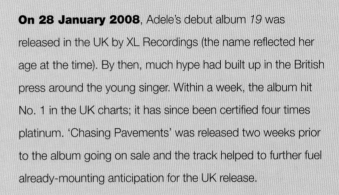

19

On 28 January 2008, Adele's debut album *19* was released in the UK by XL Recordings (the name reflected her age at the time). By then, much hype had built up in the British press around the young singer. Within a week, the album hit No. 1 in the UK charts; it has since been certified four times platinum. 'Chasing Pavements' was released two weeks prior to the album going on sale and the track helped to further fuel already-mounting anticipation for the UK release.

'Adele truly has potential to become among the most respected and inspiring international artists of her generation.'

Chuck Taylor in a Billboard review of 19

Altogether, the album features 12 tracks. Singles 'Chasing Pavements', 'Cold Shoulder', 'Hometown Glory' and the Bob Dylan cover, 'Make You Feel My Love' charted in both the US and the UK, though there was no No. 1 single. Adele has described the work as being 'modern pop' in style but it certainly has folk, jazz and soul influences. She wrote nine of the songs in a three-week period in May 2007,

> '*Heartbreak* can definitely give you a *deeper* sensibility for writing songs. *I* drew on *a lot of heartbreak* when *I* was *writing my first album – I didn't* mean to, but *I just did.*'
>
> *Adele*

following the messy break-up with her cheating first love. 'It was my first relationship,' she told *Cosmopolitan*. 'I was gutted.' Yet, suddenly she had something to write about. Two years after its initial release, however, *19* would re-enter the UK charts at No. 4 – the week Adele's second offering went on sale.

Critical Response

Not only did Adele's debut do well commercially (it has since sold 6.5 million copies), she also won high praise from the majority of critics. *The Encyclopedia of Modern Music* called *19* an 'essential' blue-eyed soul recording, while *The Guardian* gave it five stars, proclaiming Adele 'a rare singer'. *People* magazine also awarded the album top marks, describing Adele's voice as 'rich and supple, robust and sultry'. Meanwhile, *BBC Music* said many of her tracks made Lily Allen and Kate Nash 'sound every bit as ordinary as they are'.

Yet the album wasn't loved by all; some critics described Adele as a cheap Winehouse imitation who didn't live up to the hype. 'Despite the early indicators, there's precious little on the album that prevents it from collapsing under the weight of its own expectation' was *NME*'s take, whereas *Entertainment Weekly* gave it a B, opining her songs weren't as 'sharp' as Duffy's. Meanwhile, a key person likely to have something to say about the album – the ex who had inspired it – somehow managed to remain silent and anonymous.

Make You Feel My Love

Despite the ferocious three-week burst of songwriting for *19* and the raw emotional experience fuelling it, Adele says she 'never really got down what I was feeling' on the tracks. 'It wasn't that I was holding back or anything, but I just couldn't get it down. I was bitterly upset,' she explains. Salvation came when her manager Jonathan Dickins sat her down and played her Bob Dylan's 'Make You Feel My Love'. Adele loved the poetry – 'The lyrics are just amazing! [The song] is about regretting not being with someone, and it's beautiful.' In fact, she found the composition summed up exactly what she'd been trying to get across. She included the cover on her album – 'It's weird that my favourite song on my album is a cover, but I couldn't not put it on there.'

'"Daydreamer" is about this boy I was in love with, like proper in love with. He was bi and I couldn't deal with that. I get really jealous anyway, so couldn't fight with girls and boys.'

Adele

'I don't have a hole in my soul. I'm not insecure in any way. What I think it is, is, I'm really awful at saying how I feel. So I've always written it down.'

Adele

Critics' Choice

19 won the young singer a number of awards and even more nominations. Adele became the first ever winner of a new category – Critics' Choice – at the 2008 BRIT Awards and was a nominee for the prestigious Mercury Prize. She also received three BRIT nominations in 2009 for her work on the album. Adele picked up the awards for Best Jazz Act at the 2008 Urban Music Awards and the European Border Breakers Award for Best Album. Her popular track 'Chasing Pavements' alone earned eight nominations, including two Grammy nominations and four MTV Video Music award nods.

'As a kid, if I was building a castle out of Lego, I'd have to do it myself. It's the same with songs now. I like to be in control.' Adele

At the 51st Grammy Awards in 2009, Adele was nominated in four categories and took home the gongs for Best New Artist and Best Female Pop Vocal Performance. A surprising success, yet she was obviously the last person to expect herself to win, having removed her shoes and belt prior to her name being called! In 2010, the track 'Hometown Glory' received a Grammy nod. It has also featured in both British and American television shows – *Skins*, *Grey's Anatomy*, *One Tree Hill*, *Hollyoaks* and *Secret Diary of a Call Girl*. By February 2012, the album had been certified six times platinum in the UK.

Across The Pond

Adele signed a deal with Columbia Records in March 2008, yet the star's foray into the United States was not immediately successful: her singles made it into the charts but not to the top. The album itself debuted at 56. The singer didn't help matters by cancelling US tour dates for her 'An Evening With Adele' concert tour. She did so just because she wanted to spend time with her boyfriend, a decision that earned her flak and something she now regrets.

Adele was partying hard again – she has an on-off relationship with red wine and cigarettes. She blames the poor decision partly on drinking 'far too much' as the basis of her intense relationship with her boyfriend at the time – 'I couldn't bear to be without him, so I was like, OK, I'll just cancel my stuff then. I can't believe I did that – it seems so ungrateful,' Adele told *Nylon* in 2009, when revealing the real reason for the cancelled shows. She now refers to that period as her 'ELC' or Early Life Crisis after which she stopped drinking alcohol completely for a time. The star's father is a former alcoholic, so it's no wonder Adele likes to keep an eye on how much she consumes. She would go on to temporarily quit drinking again in January 2011, and again following her throat surgery.

Tonight's The Night

Yet back in October 2008, it seemed Adele's attempt to crack America had failed. Sales remained relatively subdued when compared to her runaway success at home. An appearance on *Saturday Night Live* that same month would turn out to be pivotal though. Adele performed 'Chasing Pavements' and 'Cold Shoulder' on the show. In a stroke of luck, the episode also featured an appearance by then vice-president candidate Sarah Palin. It attracted its best viewership in 14 years – reaching an audience of 17 million. Within hours of the broadcast, *19* had sold 10,000 extra copies. The next day, the album topped the iTunes chart and reached No. 11 on the *Billboard* 200, a jump of 35 places. In February 2009, it was certified gold by the Recording Industry Association of America. By February 2012, *19* had reached a new high of No. 4 and is now certified double platinum.

Dealing With Fame

Adele's world changed as she was thrust headlong into the spotlight. Suddenly she had become a headlining act – for example, at the 2008 MENCAP charity gig she had supported a year previously. Now she had to get used to giving interviews and posing for photographs. She also had to deal with her fear of performing and of flying; also her dislike of touring. There was a sudden interest in her personal life and who she was seeing, not to mention the media's obsession with her weight.

'I just kinda remember becoming a bit of a woman during that time. And I think that is definitely documented in the songs.'

Adele explains the album title, 19

Adele read about herself in magazines and read comments online – some of them nasty. Yet she refused to let them bother her. She has always pledged that she is in no danger of succumbing to the 'pressures of fame', but the sudden spotlight took some time to get used to. 'It's a death trap, this industry,' she told a reporter. 'I mean, you play to 2,000 people who adore you, then you go back to your hotel room alone. That's quite a comedown.'

Despite her on-off relationship with red wine and a struggle with cigarettes, the young star has always remained focused on professionalism and success. She claims never to have taken an illegal drug in her life. 'I want to be known for my music. I don't want to be in the press for having coke up my nose, because my nan will see it,' she once said.

'All of her songs are based on real events and real people. It can be hard for her to sing them – that's happened a few times now.'

Adele's bassist, Sam Dixon

21

Adele's second offering, 21 (again, named for the age at which she wrote it), was released in January 2011. Though still a 'break-up' album inspired by heartbreak – this time a different ex – it differs slightly in style from *19*, as it contains Nashville country and blues influences she picked up while touring the US. The new album would prove to be a much bigger hit than her debut and, by February 2012, was certified 14 times platinum at home. Success in the States was also forthcoming, with the album holding the top position in the charts longer than any other since 1990.

'Rolling In The Deep', 'Someone Like You' and 'Set Fire to the Rain' were instant chart toppers and the album hit No. 1 in 18 countries. By December 2011, it had reached over 3.4 million copies in the UK, becoming the biggest-selling album of the twenty-first century when it overtook Amy Winehouse's *Back to Black*. Adele was pleased with her songwriting, calling the tracks the 'most articulate' she had produced to date.

Rolling In The Deep

A second failed relationship, this time with a guy 10 years her senior, was the inspiration behind *21*. The ex, who has so far not been publicly named, was the one who had caused her to cancel US tour dates in 2008, yet their relationship died a fiery

'She sang it once, top-to-bottom, pitch-perfect – she didn't miss a note. I looked at the engineer, then at her and said, "Adele, I don't know what to tell you but I have never had anyone do that in 10 years!"'

Musician Ryan Tedder recalls working on the track, 'Rumour Has It'

death in 2009, just as Adele was struggling to get work on her second studio album started. The singer has said she intended to create something more upbeat, yet the initial studio sessions only resulted in one track, 'Take It All,' a love ballad written about a difficult moment in her relationship. Disillusioned, she cancelled recording dates, but when she played her boyfriend 'Take It All', this led to an argument and eventually to a messy break-up.

'Her singing was so strong and heartbreaking in the studio, it was clear something very special was happening. The musicians were inspired, all of the playing was keying off the emotion on Adele's outrageous vocal performance.' Producer Rick Rubin

Once again Adele was heartbroken, yet inspired musically. The day after the argument, she headed straight back to the studio. All notions of 'upbeat' gone, she channelled her strong emotions into songs about love and heartbreak. That first day, she felt angry about the events of the night before and was working with the producer Paul Epworth. Together, they restructured an earlier ballad that they had started working on a year previously, making it more 'aggressive' at Epworth's suggestion. The result – smash single 'Rolling In The Deep' – was born. Adele told *Rolling Stone* the title was an adaption of a street-slang term, 'roll deep' which refers to someone always looking out for you. It was how she once felt in the relationship with her ex. 'I thought that's what I was always going to have, and um, it ended up not being the case,' she told the magazine.

'People think that I'm miserable. They are really surprised when they meet me that I'm chatty and bubbly and kind of quite carefree really. I'm the total opposite of my records.' Adele

Someone Like You

'Someone Like You' is a simple piano and blue-eyed soul ballad that appears as the eleventh track on the album, yet Adele's performance of it at the 2011 BRIT Awards proved

to be career changing. All about coming to terms with the demise of a relationship the singer didn't want to end, Adele's raw, emotional, but spine-tingling performance of the break-up ballad stunned and delighted her audience. At the end, she was forced to turn away from the microphone, biting her thumb and fighting back the tears as she was given a resounding standing ovation.

Thousands downloaded the track when a live recording was uploaded for sale directly following the show. More than 5.5 million watched a YouTube upload of the performance and, by the end of the week, the single had overtaken Lady Gaga and Adele had her first ever UK No. 1.

As for the ex-boyfriend, Adele's feelings have since mellowed to the point where she allows him some credit, noting that he 'put me on the road that I'm travelling on.'

'This next one just became my first ever UK No. 1. I've had a No. 1 before, but that was in Norway – think it was 500 sales, don't take a lot. Still counts! Got a plaque on mah wall.'

Adele on stage, talking about 'Someone Like You'

Riding High

The success of 21 easily eclipsed that of *19*. Adele's sophomore offering has broken countless records and won her a host of awards, including six Grammys, two BRIT Awards and three American Music Awards. She earned mentions in the 2012 *Guinness Book of World Records* for being the first female to have two singles and two albums in the UK Top 5 simultaneously (a feat previously achieved by The Beatles in 1963) and for *21* being the first album in UK chart history to reach sales of 3 million in one year.

At the same time, she also established a new record for the most consecutive weeks at the top with a No. 1 album – 11 – beating Madonna's previously held record of 1991, as well as the most cumulative weeks at No. 1 – with a massive 21 weeks.

'When I hear artists say, "Performing is what I'm meant to do", I think, "Whaaaat?" This ain't what you're meant to do. It ain't normal.'

Adele on her stage nerves

'We would like to *reiterate* that *Adele* is to *undergo surgery* for a *haemorrhaged vocal cord.* *All* reports regarding *any other* condition are *100 per cent false.*'

Adele's spokesperson denies reports of throat cancer

Hot Property

In the US, the album has held the top position longer than any other since 1990. With the release of the third track – 'Set Fire To The Rain' – becoming Adele's third No. 1 in the US, she became the first artist in history to lead the *Billboard* 200 concurrently with three *Billboard* Hot 100 No. 1s. Adele is also the first female artist to have three singles in the Top 10 of the *Billboard* Hot 100 at the same time and the first female artist to have two albums in the Top 5 of the *Billboard* 200, with two singles in the Top 5 of the *Billboard* Hot 100 simultaneously. In 2011, *Billboard* named her Artist of the Year. Today, *21* is the longest-running No. 1 album by a female solo artist on the UK Albums Chart.

Vocal Troubles

Adele first began to experience difficulties with her voice in January 2011. She had been experiencing a series of sore throats and was onstage in Paris during a radio show when her voice 'just went'. 'It was literally like someone had pulled a curtain over it,' she explained. Adele was diagnosed with acute laryngitis but was able to continue her European tour after a couple of weeks' rest – 'I had to sit in silence for nine days, chalkboard around my neck. Like an old-school mime, like a kid in the naughty corner, like a Victorian mute.'

In May, she suffered a vocal haemorrhage – a burst blood vessel on her vocal cord. She stopped drinking and smoking,

and cut out spicy food, citrus and caffeine on medical advice. Her throat appeared to heal and so she began another round of touring. But, at her best friend's wedding on 1 October, it happened again. The singer was now forced to cancel her sell-out Adele Live tour through North America. Of course she was scared, but Adele had the finest assistance in the form of renowned throat surgeon Steven Zeitels, MD, who has worked his magic on a range of stars, including Julie Andrews, Steven Tyler and Cher. The surgeon removed a benign polyp from her vocal cord in the first week of November, following which she was forced into three weeks of silence. She issued a written statement explaining that the delicate microsurgery had been a success and thanking her loyal fans for the hundreds of messages of support she received as she recovered in private with the support of friends and family.

'I knew my voice was in trouble,' she says, 'and obviously I cried a lot. But crying is really bad for your vocal cords too!'

Adele tells it like it is to Vogue

'I was on in between Take That and Rihanna, the biggest productions of the night. All day I was thinking, this is gonna be a disaster.'

Adele on her 2011 BRITS performance

'I can do things that I never dreamed I'd be able to do. The best thing is, I now know what I want for myself and from someone else. I didn't know what I wanted before.'

Adele on her ex

Comeback Queen

'There are a lot of people who probably think that I'm never going to sing again, so I will come for them and kick their arses!' Adele joked with a reporter on the red carpet pre-Grammys. Her phenomenal success that night wasn't restricted to winning six awards though: Adele's knockout performance confirmed her famous voice had been unaffected by throat surgery.

'I have absolutely no intention of going into acting or making perfumes: I am a singer. I will stick to what I am good at, and not spread myself thin and become mediocre at everything I do.'

Adele

She has since spoken about the time following the operation in a positive light. 'I think I just needed to be silenced. And when you are silent, everyone else around you is silent,' she told *Vogue*. The singer admitted life before her voice troubles was extremely fast-paced and exhausting but that following the surgery, the noise in her life, 'just stopped'. 'It was like I

> *'I'm attentive; I'll do anything for my man. I'm a good cook, I'm funny, I always want to have sex – well, most girls don't.'*
>
> *Adele on her wifely skills*

was floating in the sea for three weeks. It was brilliant. It was my body telling me to fix me. I had so much time to kind of go over things and get over things, which is amazing. I think if I hadn't had my voice trouble, I would never have broached those subjects with myself,' she revealed. Adele admitted that as of 2012 she finally felt 'at peace' with herself, having taken the time to reflect on her achievements and to allow herself to feel proud – 'I've never fully appreciated the things that I've achieved until now.'

Cupid's Arrow

Her career may have been hanging in the balance, yet in October 2011 Adele's love life was suddenly transformed when she met new love Simon Konecki. The former Etonian and City banker founded water distribution charity, Drop4Drop and is 14 years Adele's senior. According to *The Daily Mail* the pair were introduced by mutual friends at a fundraising event, where Adele expressed interest in Konecki's work. Adele has said Konecki's support was vital to her recovery and comeback. 'He's wonderful!' she gushed. 'And he's proud of me, but he doesn't care about what I do or what other people think. He looks after me.'

In January 2012, it was widely reported that Konecki was in fact a married man. The reports were however quickly quashed by the singer in a statement – which she claimed would be 'the first and last time' any details of the relationship would be discussed. 'Contrary to the reports and headlines… Simon is divorced and has been for four years.'

'If I hadn't met him, I think I'd still be that little girl I was when I was 18. And the best thing is, I now know what I want for myself and from someone else. I didn't know what I wanted before.'

Adele no longer feels bitter towards her ex

Home Sweet Home

Around the time of the 2012 Grammys it was reported Adele had upgraded her two-bedroom Notting Hill flat to rent a Grade II-listed countryside mansion in West Sussex, not far from her lover's Brighton base. With 10 bedrooms, two swimming pools, a helicopter pad and 25 acres, the singer's manor came with a rental bill of £15,000 per month – but it was only temporary. She and Simon recently purchased a £2 million Brighton pad with seaside views, and are reportedly looking for a London 'family home' and a holiday home in Kenya, where Simon does a lot of his charity work.

The Future

Adele's third album will be a 'happy' one, she said in early 2012. She has also pledged to take more time out from her busy schedule to protect her relationship – 'If I'm constantly working, my relationships fail. At least now I have enough time to write a happy record, be in love and be happy.' She has hinted that she would like to do a Lily Allen and leave the music industry early, professing a desire to settle down. Even before the release of her second album, she listed having her own family as a top five-year goal. 'I want to settle down and have a family, definitely sooner rather than later,' she declared, before adding, 'I'd like to have finished my second album too, maybe even my third. I'd like a sound that sticks around, that other people are inspired by and that people know is me.' The singer has said she 'never' wants to leave London though – 'I love it here and I am really proud to be British.'

'I like looking nice, but I always put comfort over fashion. I don't find thin girls attractive; be happy and healthy. I've never had a problem with the way I look – I'd rather have lunch with my friends than go to a gym.'

Adele

The Look

Adele is in a league of her own when compared to the likes of Katy Perry and Lady Gaga. The differences are not limited to their music styles either. An ardent fan of comfortable elegance and the colour black, when Adele's touring, there's no need to worry about 11 costume changes and the possibility of a wardrobe malfunction. She is not your typical, ab-flashing pop princess, yet she has undoubtedly become increasingly glamorous as her fame has spread. At awards ceremonies, with advice from a team of beauty and fashion advisors, she looks as if she was born to walk the red carpet. Her hairstyles keep getting more sophisticated and at the Grammys a new blonde 'do was revealed, part of her most glamorous look yet – the attention to detail was such that even her nails had a 'Louboutin' manicure – long shimmering talons, with the underside of the tips painted a bright red as a reflection of the iconic shoes. Adele's A-list locks are looked after by Mayfair colourist Jo Hansford, whose other clients include the Duchess of Cornwall and Gwyneth Paltrow.

A Designer World

Adele's style status increased in leaps and bounds when US *Vogue* editor-in-chief and alleged ice queen Anna Wintour met the singer in 2009. She was summoned for her first major shoot, with the images captured by legendary snapper Annie Leibovitz. Before being called in to meet Wintour, Adele said

she was left waiting in a hallway. 'It was just like *The Devil Wears Prada*. I was really frightened and I went in and she was so nice.'

At that point, Adele didn't really have a favourite designer, yet Wintour was quick to point her in the right direction, style-wise. Before long, she was snapped with a series of coveted fashionista accessories – a Jimmy Choo handbag, designer shades and the like. British fashion institution Burberry is a hot favourite of Adele's, if recent choices are any indication of her look. At the BRIT Awards in 2012, her classy, full-length Burberry gown perfectly reflected the star's signature style – classic, black and elegant, with sparkle (she also wore a Burberry dress to the 2011 MTV Video Music Awards). At the 2012 Grammys, Adele shimmered in a custom-made Giorgio Armani sequined gown, accessorized with a Harry Winston ring, De Beers earrings and Christian Louboutin heels. Bold red lips completed her glamorous look.

'Even if I did have, you know, a Sports Illustrated body, I'd still wear elegant clothes. I ain't looking like no "slapper". Exploiting yourself sexually is not a good look.' Adele

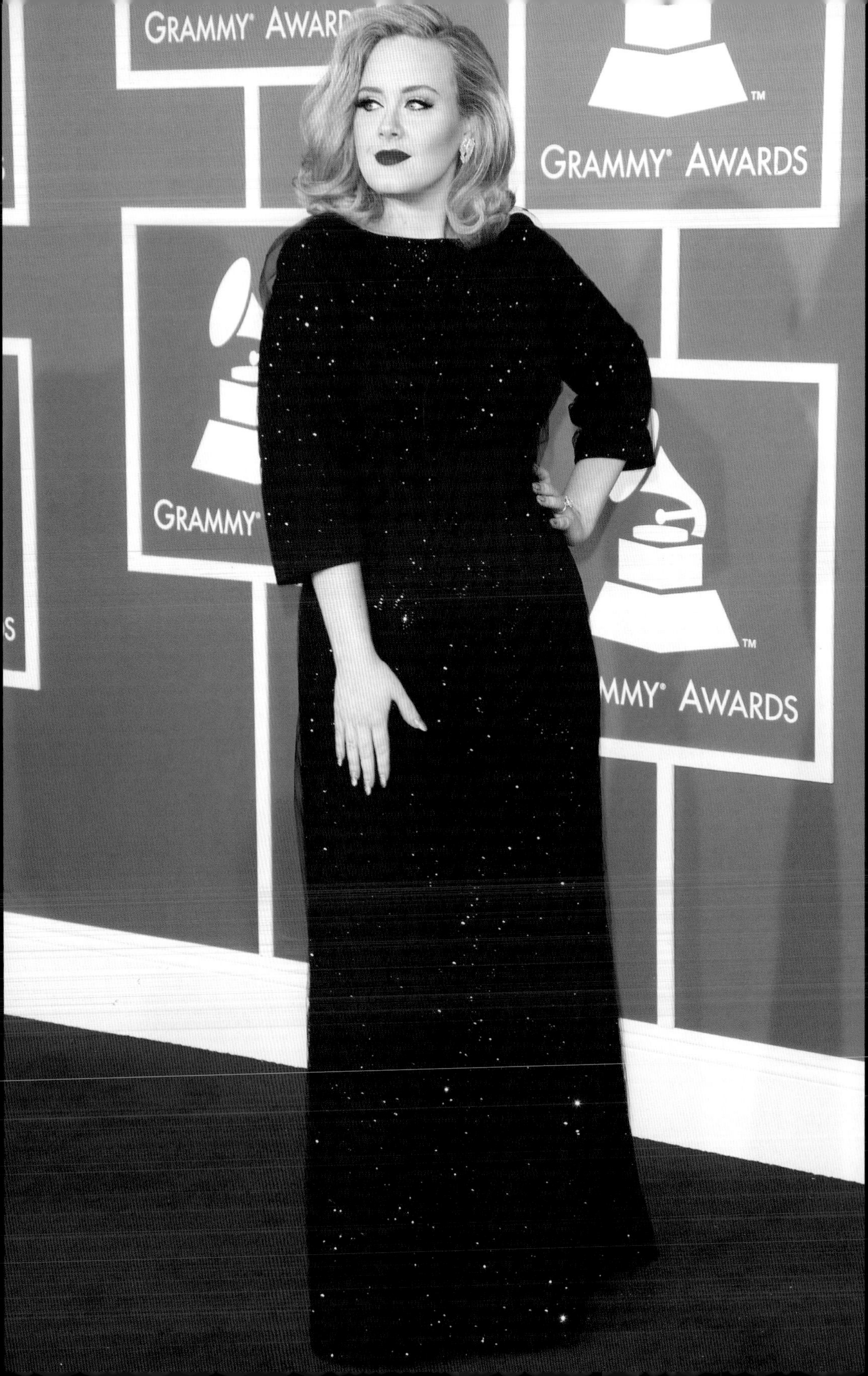
GRAMMY® AWARDS
GRAMMY® AWARDS
GRAMMY®
MMY® AWARDS

Not Bovvered!

Adele definitely breaks the skinny star stereotype. Her seeming nonchalance when it comes to her curvy size-14 figure has attracted much attention. Many see her as a positive role model – a normal-sized woman, who is self-assured and confident. Some articles have referred to her 'weight issues', however, and in 2012 Chanel designer Karl Lagerfeld raised eyebrows when he proclaimed the star, 'a little too fat.' In the same interview, he complimented her for her 'beautiful face and divine voice' and later claimed his 'fat' remark had been taken out of context, but the damage was done.

Adele herself genuinely appears not to give a damn what anybody thinks – indeed, she maintains the constant focus on her appearance continues to 'surprise' her. In an interview with *People* the day after Lagerfeld's faux pas, the singer proclaimed she has never wanted to look like a model – 'I represent the majority of women and I'm very proud of that.' In the past she has told reporters that if they ever saw her 'rail thin', she could guarantee there had to be something wrong – 'I like having my hair and face done, but I'm not going to lose weight because someone tells me to. I make music to be a musician, not to be on the cover of *Playboy*.' She was, however, looking noticeably slimmed down in 2012, attributed to the star's decision to embark on a healthier lifestyle.

'I love seeing Katy Perry's boobs and bum. Love it! But that's not what my music is about. I don't make music for eyes, I make music for ears.'

Adele

Fans

Adele has attracted a diverse, cross-generational, international legion of fans. While it was teenage girls who first clicked onto the singer via channels such as Myspace, their mothers soon grew to love her too. The star has often paid tribute to her loyal fanbase, particularly for accepting her as she is. 'To all the fans,' she trilled at the BRITS, 'no one's made me feel like I've had to be any different.' She has said it gives her a 'boost' that people dig her music and 'also seem to like me', yet she admits being in the spotlight has made her feel as though a 'boundary' has been crossed.

Having photographers hanging around outside her house for hours is not her idea of fun. Until she moved into her own flat in Notting Hill in November 2008, Adele still lived with her mother in South London. It was just as well Adele's mother later sold the place, as the 'dodgy' front door had led to Adele's most ardent fans actually climbing up onto her roof terrace.

*'I am not **moaning** about it **because** it comes with the **job**, but I can't go back to my **London house** because the **press** are **always** there.' Adele*

The Daydreamers

Adele is part of the social media generation and is perfectly at ease with it. Originally, she got noticed through Myspace, which she joined in 2004. She has said she loves blogging, and entries on her official website as well as her Twitter posts would appear to reflect this and to be the genuine work of the singer herself, rather than her promo team. By May 2012, Adele had over 5,700,000 Twitter followers. Meanwhile, her free mobile application had been downloaded by hundreds of thousands of fans. The app allows them to keep up with all her Tweets, blog posts and news while allowing them to post their own photos and comments too. Adele's die-hard online followers recently dubbed themselves 'the Daydreamers' – a term that has since caught on, being used in the media and by the singer herself.

Loved By All

It seems other celebrities can't get enough of the London lass either. Rapper Kanye West was an early convert and posted the video of 'Chasing Pavements' on his blog with the comment 'this s**t is dope'. Hollywood superstar Julia Roberts wrote a column in which she sang Adele's praises; Britney Spears has spoken of her 'love' of the star' while pop institution Kylie, who presented Adele with her BRIT Award for Best Female Artist in 2012, enthused about the singer on the red carpet. 'I love Adele,' Kylie said, going on to praise the younger singer's voice, 'humanity' and dirty jokes. 'I just think

'We feel like Adele's in our book club or she lives in our neighbourhood – that's a gift, to make people feel that way.'

Julia Roberts

she's fantastic.' Celeb blogger Perez Hilton is another in complete awe and, after the singer's 2012 Grammys performance, noted in his blog: 'Seriously, how can one person have so much talent!! It's like whenever she sings, we hear the song for the first time again!'

Former British Prime Minister Gordon Brown even sent a thank you letter to Adele in 2009. The singer said, 'It was really nice. It went, "with the troubles that the country's in financially, you're a light at the end of the tunnel."' Perhaps her most ardent famous fan is Beyoncé Knowles. The first time the stars met, Beyoncé proclaimed: 'You're amazing! When I listen to you, I feel like I'm listening to God.' She has cited Adele as one of the influences for her fourth solo album, 4, and even seemed to be thinking of the singer when naming her baby daughter Blue – Adele's middle name.

*'I am quite loud and bolshie.
I'm a big personality.
I walk into a room,
big and tall and loud.'*

Adele

'She just comes across as very approachable, just a normal English girl, and so people say hello and want to talk to her everywhere she goes.'

Rose Moon, who travels with Adele and works for her management company, tells the author

What's She Like?

Adele has cheeky, natural charm. She comes across as a lovely young woman, yet she is also known for cussing like a sailor continually. When at home, she's a bit of a clean freak and can't go to bed until everything's tidied up, describing the habit as 'really anal'. She also says that she loves cooking, a new-found skill: 'I can cook anything – lasagne, roasts, I can do pies – I can do everything.' Adele is also a self-confessed 'safety freak' – in fact the opposite of her mother, who loves adventure and, as of 2011, was really into paragliding. According to interviewers' observations over the years, it would seem the singer has a very on-off approach to drinking and smoking cigarettes. And she has admitted to being a drama queen in previous relationships. 'That's a bad thing – I can flip really quickly,' the DVD of a Royal Albert Hall gig in September 2011 records her admitting.

Adele Hearts . . .

Adele is an ardent film buff, who has said she likes watching six movies per week. She's also a big football fan and actively supports her 'hometown' (i.e North London) Premier League football club, Tottenham Hotspur. An exciting moment for Adele was bumping into the team at a Liverpool hotel. Manager Harry Redknapp failed to recognize her as she chatted away; she says he gave her 'dirty looks'. In Redknapp's defence, the chance encounter occurred before *21* was released.

'*It's important* to me that *I give,* because people always helped me and my mum out when we *needed it.*'

Adele explains why she gives to charities

Despite love for her team, Adele's favourite colour is green, the same shade as her eyes. She has said money isn't a big driver for her and she likes to support charities, including the famous children's charity, Great Ormond Street Hospital.

Did You Know?

Adele once did a cameo of herself in an episode of Channel 4's *Ugly Betty*. She has a miniature dachshund called Louis Armstrong. Previously, she has said that she hates the red carpet and it gives her stomach cramps. The singer once missed a friend's hen do to attend the VMAs in the line of duty but was 'bitter' about having to do so. She thinks *Twilight* star Robert Pattinson is hot and loves shock rappers Odd Future.

When asked what superpower she'd most like to have, she firstly said 'sharp night vision' before settling on invisibility, so that she could 'listen to people bitching or something.'

NOOOOOO!!!

One of her all-time most embarrassing moments was in 2009, at the MusicCares Person of the Year event, during a tributary performance of Neil Diamond's 'Cracklin' Rosie'. Bizarrely, Adele was observed by the audience via the big screens with a tampon stuck to her thumb. She'd improvised to stop bleeding after tearing her nail just before the gig. She hadn't realized it was visible until Anthony Keidis of The Red Hot Chili Peppers filled her in post-performance. 'It was awful!'

She has also owned up to joining an Internet dating service prior to finding love with Simon Konecki. After trying it once, she quit, explaining: 'I was drunk, upset and listening to Sinéad O'Connor's 'Nothing Compares 2 U'!'

'I do give as good as I get. I know I play the victim on the album, but pffft.... That poor boy!'

Adele shows she's over her failed romance at a gig at the Royal Albert Hall, 2011.

Further Information

Adele Info

Birth Name Adele Laurie Blue Adkins

Birth Date 5 May 1988

Birth Place London

Height 1.75 m (5 ft 9 in)

Nationality British

Hair Colour Red (ginger biscuit!);
sometimes dyed blonde

Eye Colour Green

Alter Egos Adele

Discography

Albums & EPs

19 (2008)

iTunes Live from SoHo (EP, 2009)

21 (2011)

iTunes Festival: London 2011 (EP, 2011)

Live At The Royal Albert Hall (video album, 2011,
UK No. 2, US No. 1)

Singles

2007: 'Hometown Glory'

2008: 'Chasing Pavements' (UK No. 2, US No. 1)

'Cold Shoulder'

'Make You Feel My Love' (UK No. 4)

2010: 'Rolling In The Deep' (UK No. 2, US No. 1)

'Someone Like You' (UK & US No. 1)

'Set Fire To The Rain' (US No. 1)

'Rumour Has It'

Tours

An Evening With Adele (2008–9)

Adele Live (2011)

Awards

American Music Awards

2011: Favorite Adult Contemporary Artist

Favorite Pop/Rock Female Artist

Favorite Pop/Rock Album *21*

BRIT Awards

2008: Critics Choice

2009: Best British Female

2012: Mastercard British Album of the Year *21*

BT Digital Music Awards

2011: Best Independent Artist or Group

ECHO Music Awards

2012: Rock/Pop (International Female Artist)

Album of the Year *21*

Glamour Women of the Year Awards

2009: UK Solo Artist of the Year

2011: UK Musician/Solo Artist of the Year

Grammy Awards

2009: Best New Artist

Best Female Pop Vocal Performance

'Chasing Pavements'

2012: Album of the Year *21*

Best Pop Vocal Album *21*

Record of the Year 'Rolling In The Deep'

Song of the Year 'Rolling In The Deep'

Best Short Form Music Video 'Rolling In The Deep'

Best Pop Solo Performance 'Someone Like You'

Juno Awards

2012: International Album of the Year *21*

MOBO Awards

2011: Best UK R&B/Soul Act

MTV Europe Music Awards

2011: Best UK/Ireland Act

MTV's Song of the Year

2011: 'Rolling In The Deep'

MTV Video Music Awards

2011: Best Art Direction In A Video 'Rolling In The Deep'

Best Cinematography In A Video 'Rolling In The Deep'

Best Editing In A Video 'Rolling In The Deep'

Q Awards

2011: Best Female Artist

Best Track 'Rolling In The Deep'

UK Video Music Awards

2011: Best Pop Video 'Rolling in the Deep'

Best Cinematography In A Video 'Rolling In The Deep'

Online

adele.tv

Official site with a blog, forum, news, events and links

myspace.com/adelelondon

Check this site out for Adele's latest songs, videos and awards info

xlrecordings.com/adele

Adele's official record label site at xl recordings

facebook.com/adele

Check out Adele's latest writing on the wall

twitter.com/officialadele

Join the millions of other followers @OfficialAdele

Biographies

Alice Hudson (Author)

From New Zealand, Alice fused twin passions for writing and music while a student, reviewing and interviewing international bands and DJs. She is currently based in London, writing and researching for corporate clients across a wide range of sectors, from health and fitness and financial services, to social media and entertainment. Other titles for Flame Tree include *Katy Perry: Rebel Dreamer*, *Will & Kate: Fairy Tale Romance* and *Jessie J: Keeping It Real*.

Malcolm Mackenzie (Author)

Malcolm Mackenzie is the editor of *We Love Pop*. He started as a professional pop fan writing for teen titles such as *Top of the Pops*, *Bliss* and *TV Hits* before moving into the adult market working for *GQ*, *Glamour*, *Grazia*, *Attitude*, and newspapers such as *The Times*, *The Sunday Times*, *The Guardian* and *thelondonpaper* where he was Music Editor for three years before returning to the teen sector to launch *We Love Pop*.

Picture Credits

All images © Getty Images:

Mark Allan/WireImage: 45, 114; Robyn Beck/AFP: 99; Dave M. Benett: 67, 91; Paul Bergen/Redferns: 14, 24; Gareth Cattermole: 40; Lester Cohen/WireImage: 68, 110; Mike Coppola/FilmMagic: 96; Gregg DeGuire/FilmMagic: 84; Rick Diamond/WireImage: 52; Kevork Djansezian: 12; Paul Drinkwater/NBCU Photo Bank: 102; Dana Edelson/NBC/NBCU Photo Bank: 93; Jon Furniss/WireImage: 77; Sean Gallup: 51; Rosie Greenway: 20, 78; Jo Hale: 26, 36, 54; Samir Hussein: 29, 34; Dimitrios Kambouris/WireImage: 6, 61; Peter Kramer/NBC/ NBCU Photo Bank: 22, 46; Jeff Kravitz/FilmMagic: 82, 87; Matthew J. Lee/The Boston Globe: 86; Michael Loccisano: 88, 124; Dan MacMedan/ WireImage: 4, 16, 108; Stacie McChesney/NBC/NBCU Photo Bank: 122; Eamonn McCormack/ WireImage: 56, 107; Valerie Macon/AFP: 97; Robert Marquardt: 18; Mike Marsland/WireImage: 11; Kevin Mazur/ WireImage: Cover, 49, 117; Tim Mosenfelder: 43; Leon Neal/AFP: 118; Stefan M. Prager/Redferns: 37; John Shearer/ WireImage: 70; Andy Sheppard/ Redferns: 30, 64, 120; Ben Stansall/ AFP: 74; Astrid Stawiarz: 9, 58; Greetsia Tent/WireImage: 38, 113; Mark Venema: 95; Rob Verhorst/ Redferns: 62, 73, 104; Jay West/WireImage: 32; Tim Whitby: 101; Kevin Winter: 81.